WALK ON MAPS

Mel Campbell

Rourke Publishing LLC
Vero Beach, Florida 32964

© 2007 Rourke Publishing LLC

All rights reserved. No part of this book may be reproduced or utilized in any form or by any means, electronic or mechanical including photocopying, recording, or by any information storage and retrieval system without permission in writing from the publisher.

www.rourkepublishing.com

PHOTO CREDITS: Renee Brady, Craig Lopetz, Digiphoto, Mats Lund

Title page: Renee Brady

Editor: Robert Stengard-Olliges

Cover design by Nicola Stratford.

Library of Congress Cataloging-in-Publication Data

Campbell, Mel.
 Walk on maps / Mel Campbell.
     p. cm. -- (My first math)
 Includes index.
 ISBN 1-59515-979-7 (hardcover)
 ISBN 1-59515-950-9 (paperback)
 1. Map reading--Juvenile literature. I. Title.
 GA130.C246 2007
 912.01'4--dc22
                              2006019795

Printed in the USA
CG/CG

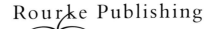

www.rourkepublishing.com – sales@rourkepublishing.com
Post Office Box 3328, Vero Beach, FL 32964

WALK ON MAPS

First Day of School	4
What is a Map?	8
What Street Should We Take?	14
Glossary	23
Index	24

First Day of School

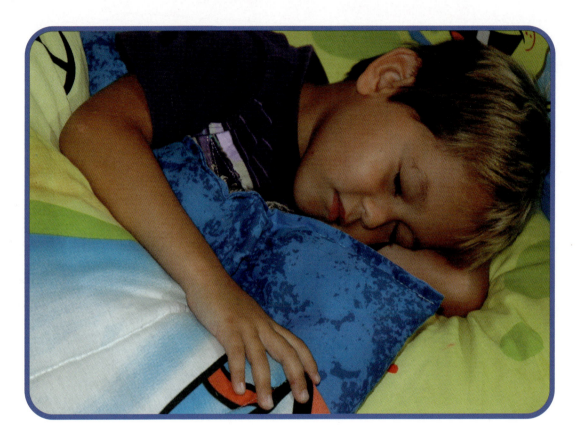

Anthony was sleeping peacefully in bed, when he heard his Dad's voice. "Time to get up. This is your first day in your new school. I have breakfast all ready for you in the kitchen."

"You don't want to be late for school on your first day. Come and eat breakfast. You need the energy to walk to school!"

Anthony said, "Walk to school? I don't know the way to my new school. Will you come with me?"

"Yes, his Dad responded, I will walk with you to school this morning. I made a **map** that will help us find your new school. Your school is not far from here."

What is a Map?

"Dad, what is a map?"

"Anthony, a map is picture to help you find where you want to go. Here is a map that I made with our home on it and your new school.

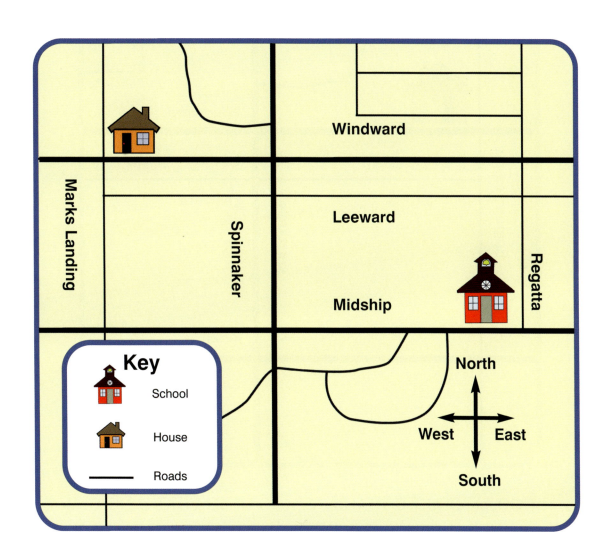

   Anthony looked carefully at the map where he saw his house and his new school.
"What are all those names on the map?" Anthony asked.

Dad answered, "Those names are the **streets**. Can you see the name of the street that our house is on?" Anthony looked carefully and said, "Marks Landing." "That name is also on a street sign," responded Dad.

Dad asked Anthony, "what's the name of the street that the school is on?" Again Anthony looked carefully and pointed to Midship and asked his dad to say the street name. "Midship," Dad responded.

"Look, Anthony, the name Midship is also on the street sign!"

What Street Should We Take?

Dad pointed to the map and said, "Let's begin our walk to you new school. What street should we take?" "Windward, of course," answered Anthony.

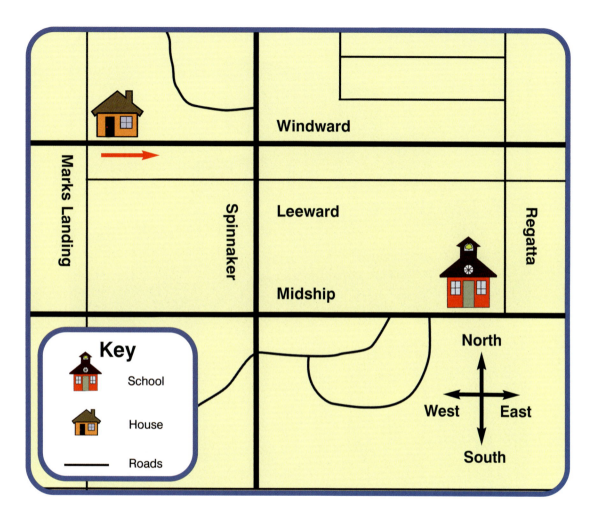

"Good, replied Dad, let me put an arrow on the map to tell us the direction to go."

Anthony and Dad walked until they came to a street named Midship.

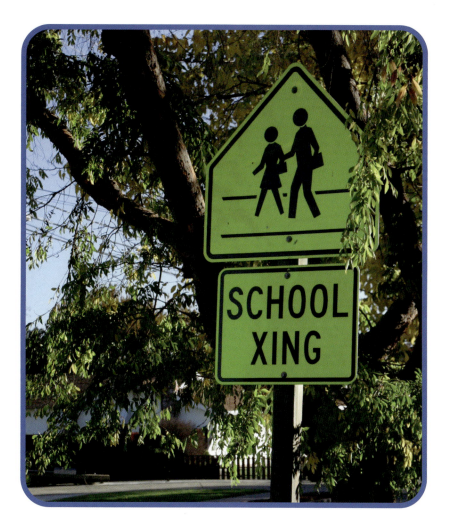

Anthony looked at the map, and then looked to the left and he could see the school sign.

"There it is my new school," he proudly said.
And sure enough there was his new school.

Anthony learned that he could find places once he had a map like this one.

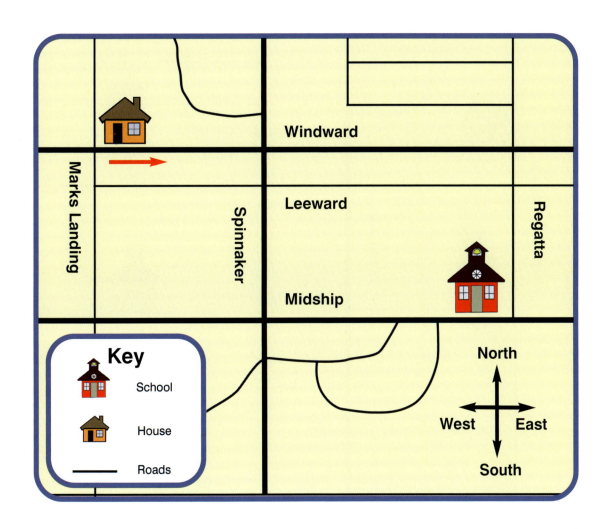

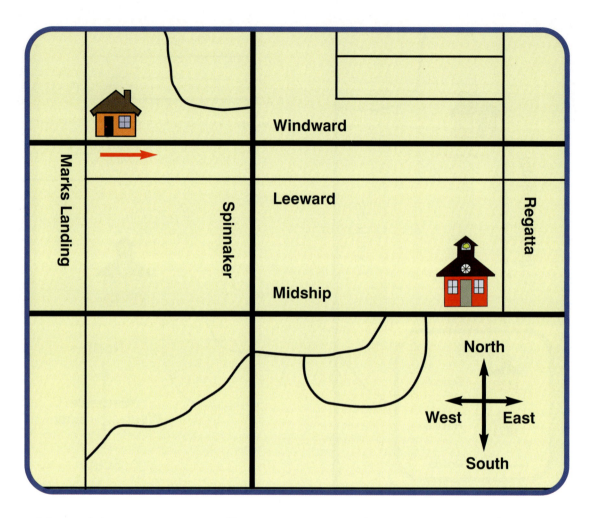

Now it's your turn. Can you use the map and find another **route** Anthony could take to get from his house to school?

Glossary

map (MAP) — a representational drawing of roads or landscape

route (ROOT) — a way to get from on place to another

street (STREET) — a roadway

Index

arrow 15
breakfast 4, 5
map 6, 8, 10, 14, 15, 17, 20, 22
walk 5, 6, 14

Further Reading

Ross, Val. *The Road to There: Mapmakers and Their Stories*. Tundra Books, 2003.
Redbank, Tennant. *Which Way, Wendy?*. Kane Press, 2005.
Wade, Mary Dodson. *Types of Maps.* Children's Press, 2003.

Websites To Visit

www.nationalgeographic.com/maps/
www.greenmap.com/ymaps/ymindex.html
www.eduplace.com/ss/maps/

About The Author

Melvin Campbell's professional career has been divided between teaching chemistry and teaching teachers to teach. In addition to his work as an university education professor he can often be found in elementary classrooms sharing his love for words in creative and dramatic ways. Dr. Campbell enjoys collecting maps and along with his wife is an avid bird watcher.